C000178328

Old Yorkshire Recipes

by

Joan Poulson

First edition October 1974
Second impression March 1975
Third impression January 1976

Published by Hendon Publishing Co. Ltd., Hendon Mill, Nelson, Lancashire.
Text © Joan Poulson 1974
Printed by Fretwell & Brian Ltd., Howden Hall, Silsden, Nr. Keighley, Yorkshire.

60p

Acknowledgements

I should like to thank all my friends and acquaintances who have made this book possible by passing on to me family recipes and allowing me to borrow books and photographs. In particular, I am very grateful to Sylvia Fergusan of Beverley, Ian Dewhurst of Keighley, Stanley Cookson of Colne and Mr. Whittleston of Harrogate for their assistance. I should also like to acknowledge the help given by the following libraries:-

Beverley, Bradford, Doncaster, Harrogate, Hull, Keighley, Scarborough, Skipton, York and the North Yorkshire County Library. I also acknowledge the help given by the staff of the Shibden Hall Museum, Halifax.

Whenever necessary, permission has been obtained to publish photographs, etc. but if copyright has been accidentally infringed in any way, I do apologise.

Introduction

IN 1865, Yorkshire was described as 'perhaps the richest county in England' and in 1663 Fuller wrote 'one may call and justify this to be the best shire of England'. Although I love Yorkshire very much, I cannot as a Lancastrian agree with this latter statement but I am wholeheartedly in accord with Speed who, in 1677 said 'This county of it-selfe is so beautiful in her own natural colours, that (without much helpe) she presents delightful varieties both to the sight and senses'.

Three hundred years later, Yorkshire still possesses some of the most lovely and varied scenery in England but now has the addition of some of the countries' greatest cities.

From the gentle, green Dales, spectacularly beautiful limestone regions, quaint sea-side villages, subtly colourful moorland areas, Yorkshire is magnificent!

The county has many traditions and, like all places which developed so much during the Industrial Revolution, these are on two levels. Firstly, and most ancient, are those traditions and customs from agricultural areas, having their origins lost in pagan times. Traditions in towns are often peculiar to one industry and are much more recent in origin. Food, also, varies between town and country areas. In the latter, dishes were cooked using locally grown ingredients, which obviously limited the scope of the cook. There is, therefore, less variety in country dishes but they are often richer since full use was made of the excellent farm produce. In towns, plainer dishes evolved—often those which could be left to cook on the hob through the day, while all the family were at work. This was the only way in which a cheap, hot meal would be ready when the tired mother returned home. Wages were low and people could no longer rely on home produced food, after moving to towns in search of work. Gradually ingredients became more assorted as shops stocked produce from all parts of the country. More elaborate and expensive dishes are also a part of Yorkshire cookery—from the homes of large landowners and, in more recent times, the houses of mill-owners, colliery-owners and businessmen of all kinds in the developing and prosperous cities of Victorian Yorkshire.

As the counties' scenery is so mixed, so is the ancestry of its people. A man wrote in 1861 'I had little difficulty in discerning among them the three principal varieties of Yorkshireman.' There was the tall, broad-shouldered rustic, whose stalwart limbs, light grey or blue eyes, yellowish hair and open features indicate the Saxon; there was the Scandinavian, less tall and big, with eyes, hair and complexion dark, and an intention in the expression not perceptible in the Saxon face; and last, the Celt, short, swarthy and Irish looking. The first two appeared to me most numerous in the East and North Ridings, the last in the West.

Celts have a great feeling for colour and beauty but are sometimes said to be unimaginative. I have usually found the opposite to be true, although the only commonly believed superstition among Celtic races seems to be that where it was believed that the 'Evil Eye' could cause one's livestock to die. An invisible evil which would affect the pocket! This is a characteristic most frequently connected with the Yorkshireman but he often has a wry joke against himself on this point. 'If tha does owt fer nowt, do it fer thisen'. This is supposed to be the motto of most Yorkshire families but I'm happy to say that it hasn't been true of the Yorkshirefolk I've met. The novelist Mrs. Gaskell did however write that the Yorkshireman of the West Riding was a 'sleuth-hound' after money.

There was always a close connection in the past between food and religious festivals. At Michaelmas every farmhouse was said to smell of sage and onion and in 1894 was written 'The Michaelmas goose is a dish without which no well-ordered dinner table on September 29th would be complete'. This custom is said to have originated in the days of Queen Elizabeth I. The story relates that she was having goose for dinner on this day and news was brought to her of the defeat of the Spanish Armada. To commemorate this great news, people decided to serve goose every year on Michaelmas Day. Although this sounds credible, the fact is that goose had been the traditional dinner for Michaelmas long before then, probably because of the custom in country districts for tenants to give a stubble goose to their land-lord when paying their rent on Michaelmas Day.

Shrovetide, often called Fastens in Yorkshire, is generally associated with pancakes, but it was customary for children to go round calling at houses on the day before this, asking 'Pray dame, a collop'. They would be given a slice from one of the sides of home-cured bacon which hung from the beams in most country homes. The bacon would provide fat in which to cook the pancakes and the day became known as Collop Monday, although later, bacon was not always given but small bags of sweets were handed out instead and children would call at as many shops and houses as possible before they went to school. This 'colloping' was supposed to end at noon but in one mill yard near Huddersfield it became customary at 12-15 on Collop Monday to throw handsful of pennies to the crowd of waiting half-timers. I think that this last occurred in 1925.

Easter was a lively time, with pace-eggers (usually boys) going round singing and acting ancient plays and being given eggs, oranges or money as presents.

Many years ago, York Minster was thrown open to everyone on Shrove Tuesday and apprentices, journeymen and others would go up one of the towers to ring the Pancake Bell. This was at 11-00 a.m. and it was customary in many Yorkshire towns, among them Pickering and Richmond. The bell-ringing signalled the closing of the schools: children ran outside shouting and laughing to hurry home for pancakes. At Heden church near Hull, this bell was rung until 1885 and all apprentices whose indentures ended within twelve months gathered in the belfry at 11-00 a.m. to take turns to ring the bell for an hour. In Whitby, the poor went from house to house begging bacon collops or other food. The master at Sedbergh Grammar School was entitled to 4½d a year from each boy, to be paid on Shrove Tuesday and to be used for the purchase of a fighting cock. In some West Riding villages it was traditional for adults to play battledore and shuttlecock in the streets on Shrove Tuesday. A man reported last century that the streets of Morley, near Leeds, were full of women and children playing this game on Shrove Tuesday.

At Whitsuntide, a feast was held in Arkengarthdale when cheese cakes were given to all visitors. These cakes are traditional throughout Yorkshire during this season, especially in Cleveland.

Much of the early development of Yorkshire took place because of the building of monasteries and the necessity for roads to connect these with each other and with available markets.

In 1145 the monks of Jervaulx were granted the right to dig iron and lead ores in the Forest of Wensleydale and to take the flesh of deer worried by wolves. These monks had special permission to set traps for wolves in their land in Westerdale and their shepherds carried horns to call for help if necessary, 'because of the wild beats and bandits'.

The insecurity of life in country areas, because of robbers and highwaymen in the Middle Ages was an important reason for the development of towns. Pickering Moors and the Hambledon Hills were avoided as retreats for outlaws. Towns developed at points on roads which were originally made for the use of monks, but poor conditions in these towns led to early deaths. Fresh meat was in short supply, conditions were insanitary and there was a lack of medicine except those herbal remedies known to monks. Many of these were later passed on as gifts in return for help given to the monks by Yorkshire families. Another gift to Yorkshire from these holy men was the knowledge of cheese-making. When Henry VIII caused the destruction of Jervaulx Abbey, the Abbot was killed and the monks scattered. In return for the hospitality they received, the monks gave the secret of making cheese. This was supposedly first called Cover Bridge Cheese, being known first by the family living near this bridge but it is now famous as Wensleydale Cheese.

Another Yorkshire speciality attributed to monks are Pontefract Cakes. The Black Friars are said to have introduced the cultivation of liquorice into Yorkshire for use in medicines. In 1760 a chemist added sweetening to the liquorice extract and discovered a sweetmeat. Pontefract Cakes are now made from liquorice extract, treacle, sugar, flour, glucose and water.

Treacle is used in many traditional Yorkshire foods, such as parkin, gingerbread and plot toffee. A treacle posset was often drunk at night in country areas.

Good, filling meals were an essential part of country life, not only as a means of sustaining energy but to provide a chance to meet friends, neighbours and fellow-workers. A meal provided by the farmer was often the only time farmhands would eat fresh meat. A diary of 1796 refers to a farmers' wife allowing the shepherd to keep the meat from a sheep which had been killed in an accident. She wrote that it was many months since he had last eaten meat.

A great chasm existed between rich and poor and the Quakers were among those who, in the 18th century, tried to improve the lives of working people in Yorkshire and other counties. Charles Lamb wrote 'Get the writings of John Woolman by heart and so learn to love the Quakers'. The 19th century was even worse for the poor. This was the time of the 'barley war' when meal cost 5d a pound and a hard days' work earned only 10d. The better-off working-class family might be able to afford bacon and potatoes for their main meal, with porridge for breakfast but the poor suffered terribly. They were said to cook a double amount of porridge in the morning to save fuel. After breakfast, the remaining food was poured into a large, stone bottle which was corked and put into bed where it kept warm until the midday meal. They might then have oatbread for their evening meal with mint tea sweetened with treacle. A step down from this was 'porridge and stop'. All the meal left in the house was cooked for the family to eat and after this, they stopped eating until they could afford to buy more food.

When a variety of food was obtainable, many of the substantial and tasty Yorkshire dishes were evolved. Yorkshiremen in all parts of this great county are renowned as good trenchermen and last century a typical days diet for a Dales farmer might be oatmeal porridge, with plenty of milk, for both breakfast and supper; dinner started with Yorkshire Pudding—often called the 'sheet anchor' of a Yorkshireman's dinner, filling him before the meat course, then beef with perhaps two vegetables, or instead of beef the very popular ham and eggs. A story tells how a new doctor arrived in a Dales village, but after a few months was forced to leave as he could not make a living. He said that the local people were never in need of a doctor as they applied a hot poultice inside their stomachs both morning and night and so were never ill.

Country areas were usually better able to survive times of depression than the industrial areas and it is in these rural places that many old customs, connected with food, have been retained.

In farmhouses at Christmas-time, anyone who had visited the farm, for any reason, during the previous year was welcome to call for a 'Christmas pot'. This was invariably a piece of spice cake or Yule cake, with cheese and mulled ale.

It was also traditional at Christmas to serve frumenty, pepper-cake and mince pies. Visitors during the week following Christmas Day were often given a slice of this pepper cake, or spiced ginger cake with a glass of home-made wine and specially made cheese which was marked with a cross. Also traditional was Yorkshire Spice Bread which varies slightly in different districts. In Ripon it is called Ripon Spice Bread and when made at Christmas was called Yule Bread.

Other occasions when people gathered together, perhaps for the first time in a year, were village feast days. These were held annually, to celebrate the churchs' patron saints' day. After the service in church, there would be sports, dancing and an enormous 'sit-down' tea.

Funerals were also considered to be opportunities for feasting and there were quite often different foods for the different classes who might attend the funeral or just call to pay their respects. If a prosperous farmer died, his workers would be invited into the back kitchen to eat bread and cheese and drink ale. Neighbours would sit in the front kitchen with cake and ale or spirits, while the parlour was reserved for any local gentry who might call. They would be offered the best wine in the house with cake. Less socially conscious families would usually invite every member of the family and all friends and neighbours to a large tea which would be the best 'spread' it was possible to afford. It was thought to be most respectable at one time to be 'buried with boiled ham'.

In the Keighley area and along the Worth Valley, long before the Brontes brought fame to the area, funeral feasts were known as Arvills and tended to be large gatherings, often ending in fighting and drunkenness.

Funerals were commonplace among the poor and in the 19th century, when people moved to the industrial centres for work, accidents in the mines and the newly opened factories made grief and tragedy constant companions in working-class homes. In 1861, a Yorkshire newspaper reported 'This year opened with a very severe frost and the outdoor working classes suffered great privations in consequence'. The same newspaper reported 104 men and boys killed in 1862 in ironworks and coal-mines in Yorkshire, many more being severely injured.

Other newswrothy items of the period were:-

"February 9th 1864. Isaac Holden Esq. cut the first sod of the Keighley and Worth Railway at Haworth. This caused the primitive old town to be the scene of unusual bustle and gaiety. The bells rang out merrily and flags, banners and streamers were flaunted from the church tower, house tops and windows. There was a great procession and not fewer than 20,000 people covered the hills around.

June 29th 1864. A splendid new orphanage at Skircoat, Halifax, admitted the first 6 boys on this day. This is the most stately edifice that Halifax can boast and will sleep upward of 400 children between the ages of 2 and 10 or up to 12 years in special circumstances. There is a disqualification rule that no child shall be admitted who is blind, deaf, dumb, subject to fits, helplessly lame, or in any respect seriously crippled, paralysed, unable to retain urine or suffers from any infectious, contagious or incurable disease. And no child who has not been born in wedlock, or who has been a resident pauper in a workhouse.

September 17th 1864. Halifax is among the earliest of English provincial towns and possibly the first in Yorkshire to have its statue of 'Albert the Good'. It was unveiled this day and has cost 1300 guineas."

These two latter entries almost typify life in Victorian England. The orphanage must have been very welcome and certainly a great charity but to qualify for care there, a child needed a full birth certificate, excellent health and no taint of the workhouse. Difficult conditions for a poor orphan in the mid-19th century—but, respectability was every-thing! A cradle song of the period goes:-

'Hush a bye baby
Be still wi' thi' daddy,
Thi' mammy has gone to the mill.
But when she comes back,
She'll gi' thi' some pap,
Hush a bye babby, be still.'

It was a fact of life that mothers worked as soon as possible after a childs' birth. The baby would have to wait to be fed until she was able to return during a meal break and the father would work on a different shift. Since older children were also at work, the family would be unable to spend much time together, but despite, or maybe because of, all their difficulties, there was great family loyalty and closeness.

Yorkshire people have a richly diverse inheritance which has given to the elderly, who have experienced so many facets of life, a quiet strength that refuses to be hurried or flustered. They come from hard-working and God-fearing stock—which explains the old Yorkshirewoman's reply when told her religion was a crutch—'Mebbe, lad, but ah knaw as ah'm a cripple wi'out God'.

Dialect is not often heard now, but in 1861, a traveller in Yorkshire wrote that he had proof that dialect was not 'rapidly disappearing before the facilities for travel afforded by railways.' He also remarked on the rudeness, not to say coarseness of manners' of people living north of Coventry, but continues 'Generally speaking the rudeness is a safety valve that lets off the faults or seeming faults of character; and I for one prefer rudeness to that over-refinement prevalent in Middlesex, where you may not call things by their right names, and where, as a consequence, the sense of what is fraudulent, and criminal, and wicked, has become weakened, because of the very mild and innocent words in which 'good society' required that dishonesty and sin should be spoken of.'

A book written on Craven dialect in 1824 also referred to 'good society' in the following way 'They sud first send missionaries amaang gentlefolk i' England to larn em to keep Sabbath day hoaly: and not to break it as they do by rawking abart fra place to place and keeping t'haal coutri in an uproar.'

A pity that the habits of early 19th century gentlefolk and inhabitants of Middlesex have infected us all.

Many recipes in my book come from a time when money and free time were scarce, so whatever there was became doubly precious. Most have been included just as they were given to me; untried and untested in a modern kitchen but offered in the hope that you find them as interesting as I did. Perhaps you will try them out and enjoy experimenting with a recipe that may not have been used for many years, and good luck!

Yorkshire Pudding

Yorkshire Pudding was frequently served with gravy before the main course but is also the traditional accompaniment to roast beef.

In the past, the joint was hung from a jack before the fire. A strong tin table beneath it had a hollowed centre to hold the gravy which was used to baste the beef. The pudding batter was poured into shallow dishes, or dripping pans, which were placed upon the table. These were moved around closer or away from the fire as they required cooking. Also to catch more dripping or gravy from the joint.

The pudding should be light, with crisp edges, melting in the mouth. Yorkshire people all have their own method, including special family traditions to follow, to ensure a light pudding. Young cooks are often put off by the suggested complications in making Yorkshire Pudding—it must be made several hours before you cook it; it must only be made with water; a mixture of milk and water will give the necessary lightness; whisk it thoroughly; never whisk, beat it well with a fork; etc. etc. etc. There must be more contradictory statements concerning the method of making this very simple dish than any other, when really it is just a question of making it to suit the tastes of your family. I admit that for some years we liked it heavy and stodgy—because that was the only way I could make it! Then, I discovered that my chief mistake had been in making the batter too thick. The recipe I now use does give a light, crisp-edged Yorkshire Pudding, delicious with well flavoured beef gravy–and roast beef too for special occasions! For four people—

3 oz plain flour	1 egg
$\frac{1}{2}$ pint milk	1 level teaspoon salt

Whisk the egg well, add a little of the milk and work in the flour gradually. Beat well with a fork or holed straining spoon (or any large spoon).

Add the remaining milk and either use at once or leave an hour or two until required. In a baking tin (about 8″ square), heat some dripping in the oven until very hot. I also like to include some of the beef juice from the roasting tin. Pour in the batter and cook in a hot oven, about 425° until well risen and golden brown.

Yorkshire Rarebit

Grate some cheese into a bowl and put over a pan of simmering water until it melts. Add a little pepper and salt and some dry mustard. Slowly stir in some stout and add a dash of sauce such as Worcestershire. Have ready some hot toast, pour on the cheese and top with a thick slice of grilled or boiled bacon and a poached egg.

Tipsy Cake

1 large stale sponge cake	½ pint fresh, double cream
1 pint of thick, rich custard	Blanched or lightly
Sufficient sherry to soak the	roasted almonds
cake	Apricot jam
1 small glass of brandy	Glace cherries (optional)
(optional)	Strips of angelica
	(optional)

Split the cake and spread with a good layer of jam. Put the two halves together in a glass dish and carefully pour over the sherry and brandy. Leave to soak for about an hour then cover with the cooled custard. Garnish with the cherries and angelica or with the almonds cut into long splinters and stuck all over. Decorate lavishly with thick cream.

Tipsy cake is more typical if the cake is baked in a basin, but it must then be split into extra layers to be spread with jam.

An item from the Court Rolls of the Manor of Haworth in 1708 states 'if any person or persons of the parish of Bingley shall get any turves or fuel on the commons or wastes belonging the Manor of Haworth, or lead or carry such away, or that shall suffer or permit their cattle to pasture on the said commons either summer or winter we lay a pain upon every such offender in the sum of X shillings.'

The photograph opposite was taken during the decade of the French Revolution and of the great Gold Rush of America, when many people emigrated from England to seek their fortunes in California.

Shrovetide Fritters (a recipe from Haworth)

These were traditionally made every Collop Monday, the day before Shrove Tuesday. This was a very important day in the past, when children were up early to go out 'colloping'. One phrase used when they went round the shops was—

"Pray, dame, a collop,
Or we'll give you a whallop"

Method—Rub a little lard into a pound of flour, then add some mixed spice salt and nutmeg. Stir in 4 oz. sugar, 4 oz. currants and 4 oz. sultanas. Beat 4 eggs and mix them in with 1 oz. yeast. Mix to a batter with milk and leave to stand for 2 hours. Drop from the tip of a wooden spoon into very hot fat in a frying pan. Turn and brown the other side, then drain and eat hot, sprinkled with castor sugar.

Haworth Parsonage during the 1840s.
This is one of the oldest known photographs of Haworth and was taken while the Brontë family lived there. It is known that by the 1850s the grassed area in the foreground was much more encroached upon by gravestones.

Harslet

Simply, and traditionally, a pigs' fry, liver, sweet-breads, heart, etc. sliced, seasoned and mixed with oatmeal. Then rolled in the skin which surrounds the suet and baked. Most farmers wives had their own version of harslet, or haslet, including different herbs and spices. One recipe I was given included pigs' liver, lights, heart and sweetbread with a mixture of fat and lean pork. This was either cut up finely or minced altogether and a finely chopped onion added. Seasoning and sage were added to taste then the mixture put into a caul and stitched up tightly. It was then roasted either hanging before the fire or in the oven beside it.

One Skipton butcher has been using the same recipe for harslet since 1927, his father having come to the town from Whitby early this century. He uses raw pork, with a little beef for colour and flavour, seasoning and herbs. This is all minced to a sausagemeat consistency, packed into a skin (the large intestine of a cow) and roasted. Apparently, it is becoming increasingly difficult to obtain the skins. Whatever happened to the interior of the cow in the 1970s—pre-packed plastic?

Skipton Pudding

1 teacupful flour	1 oz sugar
1 level teaspoon baking powder	2 tablespoons jam
1½ oz butter	½ teaspoon bicarbonate of soda

Put the flour, baking powder and sugar in a basin. Melt the butter and add with the jam. Dissolve the bicarbonate of soda in half a cup of warm milk and add. Steam for 2½ hours and serve with rich custard.

This is an economical pudding, but light and was described in the old, handwritten book I took it from as a 'Great favourite'.

The Craven area was originally noted for long-horned cattle than later, Short-horns were introduced. In this photograph of Skipton High Street taken on market day sometime at the turn of the century, this is the only breed of cattle to be seen. The street is milling with men and cattle with only one woman in sight and no traffic at all.

Skipton is the market town of the Craven district, which has long been a part of Yorkshire famous for cheese-making. In 1310, 147 stones of cheese from ewes milk were eaten in Bolton-in-Craven.

Cheese was the only method of storing milk and in the late 13th century cheese from ewes milk was regularly made in monasteries. Much later, milk from the cows was used to make cheese on farms but in late Victorian times, factory methods were introduced.

Whanghy cheese was made either from half skimmed milk and half 'new' or entirely from skimmed milk. Because of the lack of butterfat the cheese was hard and dry and only suitable for cooking. Its' name became a symbol for toughness.

Skipton High Street

Yorkshire Christmas Pie

In the 18th century, these pies were specially made in Yorkshire at Christmas-time and as well as being the most spectacular feature of banquets in this county, they were sometimes sent to London where they provided the talking-point at such places as the Guildhall. They were very large and heavy and a waggon carrying one as a present from Sheffiield to the Lord Chancellor in 1832, was delayed after breaking down.

The pies consisted of boned poultry, fitted one inside the other, all within an extra thick pastry case. Sometimes, the birds were partly cooked before being put into the pie.

A typical, and very old recipe—'One turkey, one goose, one fowl, one pigeon, a little sausage meat, some forcemeat, six or eight hardboiled eggs, half an ounce of pepper, half an ounce of salt, some good gravy or jelly, raised pie crust.

Bone all of the birds and season the inside of each one with pepper and salt. Put the goose inside the turkey, the fowl inside the goose and the pigeon inside that, filling the interstices with some forcemeat, the sausagemeat and the hard-boiled eggs, each cut into quarters. Sew up the turkey to give it the appearance of a whole bird and then lay it in a thick, raised crust. Cut or mark out a lid at the top, brush it over with some beaten egg-talk and ornament the top and sides. Bake it in a slow oven for some four hours, according to the size of the pie, then carefully raise the lid and pour in some savoury gravy or jelly. Let it stand to cool. When cold, seal the hole in the top with butter.

This will keep a long time as the pastry is not meant to be eaten, merely to provide a container.

The Factory Acts of 1833 and 1844 regulated the hours that children could work and laid down a minimum age. The following extract is taken from a certificate of age for a child seeking employment in the factory of Mr. William Lund of the North Becks Mill, Keighley,—

'I William Bell Sewell of High Street, duly appointed a Certifying Surgeon do hereby certify, that————, residing in————has been personally examined by me, this————day of————One thousand eight hundred and fifty————; and that the said Child has the ordinary Strength and Appearance of a child at least Eight years; and that the said Child is not incapacitated, by disease or bodily Infirmity, from working daily in the above named Factory for the time allowed by this Act.'

Harvest Buns

1 oz yeast	1 lb wholemeal flour
1 teaspoon sugar	2 oz seedless raisins
½ pint milk	2 oz castor sugar
2 oz butter	

Sieve the flour and salt. Put half into a warm bowl. Leave the yeast, 1 teaspoon of sugar and a little of the milk (first heated until blood-heat) in a bowl in a warm place until liquid. Melt the butter and add to the yeast mixture. Pour all this into the flour, beat well and put into a warm place with a cloth on top for 30 minutes. Gradually stir in the remaining flour with the fruit and sugar. Knead for a few minutes then divide into small balls (about 24) and put onto a greased tray. Again, leave in a warm place with a cloth to cover, for 40 minutes then bake in a fairly hot oven 425° 10-15 minutes.

Lemon Pudding

2 oz flour	1 egg
2 oz breadcrumbs (fresh)	1 lemon
4 oz shredded suet	½ teacupful milk
2 oz sugar	2 tablespoons syrup

Grate the lemon rind and mix into the flour, breadcrumbs and suet. Beat the eggs and add with the lemon juice, sugar and finally the milk. Beat the mixture together thoroughly and put into a buttered basin. Steam for 2 hours then turn out. This pudding looks most appetising presented in a shallow bowl, decorated with twists of lemon slices and surrounded by a steaming hot, tangy lemon sauce. It is, however, light and delicious and a good family pudding enjoyed by children when eaten with custard.

Flannel Cakes

8 oz flour	2 eggs
½ level teaspoon bicarbonate of soda	¾ pint milk
1 oz castor sugar	knob of butter the size of a walnut
¼ teaspoon salt	

Sift together the dry ingredients, rub in the butter and add the sugar. Separate the eggs and put the yolks into the mixture then gradually add the milk being careful to keep free of lumps. Whisk the egg whites until stiff and stir in lightly. Grease a frying pan and coat it thinly with batter. Cook until it bubbles on the surface, turn and cook the other side. This mixture should make 10 cakes. Keep warm, heaped on a dish and serve at once with warmed strawberry jam poured over. The sooner these are served the better as they are lightest when just cooked.

The jam is better for being diluted slightly with water —sweet white wine being a further improvement; and to place a large bowl of thick cream beside the plate of flannel cakes really lifts this simple recipe into the most tempting, mouth-watering and attractive of dishes— and forget the calories!

Lemon Sauce

1 large lemon	½ oz flour
1 oz butter	1 or 2 egg yolks
1½ tablespoons sugar	¼ pint water

Grate the rind into the sugar. Melt the butter, stir in the flour gradually then add the water a little at a time and stir continuously until the mixture comes to the boil. Simmer slowly 2 or 3 minutes. Add the sugar and lemon juice. Remove from the heat and stir in the yolks.

Yorkshire Parkin

8 oz plain flour	1 egg
8 oz medium oatmeal	$\frac{1}{4}$ pint milk
8 oz treacle (or treacle and syrup mixed)	1 level teaspoon ginger
4 oz soft brown sugar	$\frac{1}{2}$ teaspoon bicarbonate of soda
4 oz lard and butter mixed	

Melt the sugar, lard and treacle over a low heat. Beat the egg well and add to the treacle mixture with some of the milk. Put the oatmeal, flour and ginger into a large bowl and pour in the treacle, etc. Beat well then add the bicarbonate of soda, dissolved in the remaining milk, Stir well then pour into a well greased tin, about 11″ by 9″ and 2″ deep. cook at once in a moderate oven until firm, about one hour.

Another very old recipe which makes several cakes but could of course be halved. I reproduce it just as it was passed on to me by a lady in her eighties.

1 lb. fine oatmeal	$2\frac{1}{2}$ lb. treacle
1 lb. medium oatmeal	3 small teaspoons of baking soda
6 oz butter	2 eggs
6 oz lard	$\frac{1}{2}$ oz ground ginger
1 lb flour	$\frac{1}{2}$ oz ground ginger
	Beer

Sift the flour and ginger into a basin, then mix in the oatmeal. Rub in the butter and lard then stir in the warmed treacle. Lastly, dissolve the soda in half a glass of beer, then mix it into the other ingredients. The dough should be dry enough to fall in drops. It must not run. Turn into well buttered cake tins, but only fill them three-quarters full. Cook slowly until firm.

Cheese Muffins from Keighley

$1\frac{1}{2}$ cupful of flours	1 egg
4 level teaspoons baking powder	$\frac{3}{4}$ cup milk
$\frac{1}{2}$ cup grated cheese	a good pinch of salt

Mix the flour, salt, cheese and baking powder together. Beat the eggs, add to the milk then pour into the dry ingredients. Knead lightly and roll out. Cut into rounds and bake until brown in a hot oven, about 10 minutes. Best eaten while hot, split and buttered.

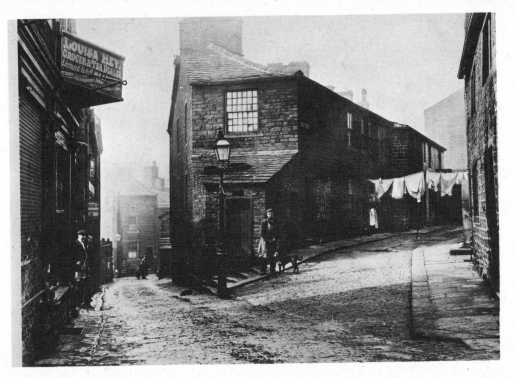

Baptist Square, Keighley, 1898.

In 1853, this area was described as containing 'filthy and offensive premises, from several privies and ash places.' These are the districts where progress and development have been essential and Keighley is rightly proud of its modern amenities but people have been far-sighted enough to retain certain old buildings of valuable historic interest.

The man in the centre of the photograph had his dog muzzled to comply with the regulations, since there was a rabies scare at the time.

Yorkshire Curd Tarts or Cheese Cakes

8 oz curds

2 eggs

4 oz sugar

2 oz currants

A small knob of butter (melted)

A little grated lemon rind

A pinch of nutmeg

Shortcrust pastry

Mix the curds with the dried fruit and flavourings. Beat the eggs well and stir in with the sugar and butter. Line a dish or plate with the pastry and put in the curd mixture. Bake in a moderate oven for 20 minutes or until set.

These tarts were traditionally served at Whitsuntide.

Curds

Heat a pint of milk until almost at boiling point then add a tablespoon of lemon juice. Remove from the heat and stir until it curdles. If thick curds have not formed, leave overnight in a warm place, covered. Strain off the whey through fine muslin, leaving behind the curds.

Curds can also be made using rennet, which can be bought from chemists' shops.

Scarborough Pudding

3 oz tapioca

3 oz sugar

8 oz red plums

1 pint water

Wash and drain the tapioca. Put into a buttered pie-dish with the sugar and water. Halve the plums, stone them and add to the other ingredients. Cook in a moderate oven for 1 hour and serve with cream.

Scarborough Castle was built in the time of King Stephen, on a high rock close to the sea and when Edward II was king he took refuge there since it was then considered to be the strongest castle in the kingdom.

This is a very good photograph of Scarborough beach early this century, since it shows so many details of working life at the sea-side, when holidays there were becoming commonplace among richer families. One or two women are selling fish, and dressed in hats and shawls despite the sunshine. A woman can be seen carrying the trestle across for her table, ready to start work and advertised for sale are 'Oysters Fresh From The Beds.'

Huddersfield Hare

This was recommended as making any tough beef taste as good as hare. Cut the beef into strips and roll in a mixture of flour, pepper add a sprinkle of nutmeg. Melt good dripping in a shallow pan and fry the pieces of beef until golden brown on all sides. Have ready a deep oven dish and put the beef into this, then an onion, stuck with about four cloves, some chopped celery, mushrooms, carrots and turnips. Add very little liquid—perhaps two tablespoons each of water and red wine. Put on a tight fitting lid and cook slowly for 2½ hours approximately at 325°.

Barley Water

2 oz pearl barley   sugar to taste
1 lemon

Put the barley in a pan, just cover with water and bring to the boil. Throw away the water, put the barley in a jug and pour over some freshly boiling water. Cover and leave for fifteen minutes. Peel a lemon very thinly and put into a bowl with some sugar. Pour boiling water onto the peel and sugar, stir well until the sugar dissolves. Leave this for 15 minutes then pour into the barley water and squeeze in the lemon juice. Leave in a cool place and strain when cold.

Baked Onions

Peel and cut the ends from large onions. Place in salted water, bring to the boil, cover and simmer for 15 minutes. Strain off the liquid (use in soup) and put the onions into a deep baking dish. Pour in beef stock to cover or come ¾ way up the onions. Put on a lid and bake 30 minutes or until tender 375°.

On Dec. 30th 1829, a large wild swan was shot near Huddersfield which measured 8′ 6″ from the tip of one wing to the other and 3′ 6″ from beak to tail. When skinned and cooked it provided a meal for 21 persons.

Huddersfield is not only famous as a great wool town but as a musical centre, being the home of the now world-famous Huddersfield Choral Society which was founded in 1836.

A view of the cobbled Westgate in Huddersfield with the two policemen seeming to be posing for the photographer.

Ripon Spice Bread

1 lb plain flour	1 level teaspoon sugar
4 oz butter	½ oz fresh yeast
4 oz lard	5 oz sugar
1 egg	¾ pint milk
8 oz mixed dry fruit	2 level teaspoons mixed
1 oz candied peel	spice
	a good pinch of salt

Put the flour and salt in a large bowl in a warm place. Cream the yeast with the teaspoonful of sugar, beat the egg and mix these together. Warm the milk to blood heat and stir into the flour with the yeast mixture. Mix well, cover with a slightly dampened cloth and leave in a warm place for an hour. Turn out and knead thoroughly working in the fruit, peel, sugar and spices. Put into two buttered, floured 1 lb tins. Leave, covered, in a warm place for 25 minutes. Bake in a hot oven, 450° or gas Mark 8, for 10 minutes then reduce to a moderate heat, 350° gas Mark 4 for approximately 50 minutes.

Apple Cake

Traditionally made in Ripon during Wilfra Week in August. This week commemorated St. Wilfred, the patron saint of Ripon Cathedral. It was also customary that week for women to put an oval dish of lemoncheese or jam tarts just inside their front doors. Passers-by were invited to help themselves.

Line a tin with pastry. Peel and thinly slice some cooking apples and put onto the pastry to a depth of ¾". cover with sugar or syrup, then sprinkle with grated cheese. Top with pastry, sealing the edges. Bake in a fairly hot oven 425 until cooked.

An old Yorkshire saying goes—

'An apple pie without some cheese
Is like a kiss without a squeeze'

Ripon market in 1905, when wealthy women were becoming more emancipated and actually played tennis and cycled in public. Notice The Oil Kings advertisement in the left foreground for Carriage Oil, Spindle Oil and Harness Oil.

There was a tradition in Ripon that immediately after morning service on Easter Sunday, the youths took away the girls' shoe buckles and returned them on Easter Monday. Then the girls retaliated, to return the buckles the following day. At one time, anyone travelling through Ripon at Eastertime would have his spurs taken away unless he paid a fine.

York Fingers

4 oz Wensleydale cheese
4 oz flaky pastry
horseradish sauce
some extra cheese, finely grated

Roll out the pastry thinly and put the 4 oz cheese in fine slices over half. Fold the other half of the pastry over the cheese and press down the edges. Roll out again and cut into small fingers. Spread with horseradish sauce and sprinkle with the grated cheese. Bake in a hot oven 450° until golden and well risen.

Yorkshire Teacakes

1½ lb plain flour	½ teaspoon salt
1 oz yeast	2 oz sugar
¾ pint milk and water mixed	2 oz lard

Put the flour and salt into a warm bowl and rub in the lard. Cream the yeast and sugar and warm the milk to blood heat. Mix the yeast and sugar into the milk then pour into the flour mixture add mix well. Leave in a warm place, covered with a slightly dampened cloth, for half an hour. Divide into 12 or 14 pieces, shape and put on warm greased tins. Cover again and leave a further half hour. Bake in a hot oven until cooked— approximately 10 minutes.

Brown Caudle of 1850. For a feverish cold.

Warm two quarts of gruel made from oatmeal or groats with a blade or two of mace and a piece of lemon peel. Strain it and stir till cold. When to be used, add a pint of good ale that is not bitter to each quart of gruel, with a gill of wine, sugar to the palate and warm together.

York is one of the loveliest cities in England with a wealth of historical interest including the magnificent Minster. In 1405 a glazier, John Thrornton of Coventry contracted with the dean and chapter of York to glaze and paint the great eastern window. The work was to be finished in three years; payment being 4 shillings a week with £5 at the end of each year. Finally, if the work was done satisfactorily he would receive £10 in silver.

York Racecourse was laid out on Knavesmire in 1730, where people had also gathered in their hundreds to watch public hangings, including that of the highwayman Dick Turpin.

A view of Parliament Street, York in 1889 showing the market. This is a busy scene and rather unusual in that there appear to be more men than women around the stalls. Notice, too, the variety of baskets in the photograph—carried, beneath the stalls and on the cart to the right. Now we are much more accustomed to seeing shopping bags and cardboard boxes.

Yarm Fair about 1920 when this was a very popular fair being attended by people from far afield to trade and barter.

Moggy

This recipe can be found in many old recipe books and perhaps the name is taken from the Old Norse language, where a heap of corn was known as Mugi. The word can also be traced back through Early English where corn was referred to as Muge and later as Muga.

1½ lb plain flour	8 oz syrup
3 teaspoons baking powder	8 oz sugar
6 oz lard	salt
6 oz margarine	milk

Mix together the flour, salt and baking powder. Rub in the fats, add the sugar and syrup. Mix to a stiff dough with milk. Shape into two pieces 1½" thick. Place on a greased baking tin and bake in a moderate oven for about 25 minutes, until firm and light brown. Cut and serve thickly buttered.

Lambs Tail Pie

When lambs' tails are docked, for hygienic reasons, they are cleaned and trimmed of the longest wool then scalded by immersing in very hot water. After a few minutes, the remaining wool is easily removed. The tails are then cut into small pieces and put into a pie-dish with some mint and seasoning. This is all covered with a crust of short-pastry which was often made using mutton fat in past times. The dish is put into a moderate oven and cooked until the meat is tender and the pastry browned. If the tails are fairly large they are stewed first with carrots and onions before being put into the pie-dish.

Two cheeses once famous in Yorkshire were Cotherstone and Cleveland cheeses. On Emmanuel Bowens' map of North Yorkshire dated 1777, is the note—'Cleveland or Cliveland in the Clay, so call'd from the high rocks and precipieces with which the parts abound and soil being of an exceeding clammy stiff clay. Here is made very good Cheese, not inferior to that of Gloucestershire.'

Darley Street, Bradford early this century with the pavements quite full of shoppers.

A 'Delicious Hash' from Bradford

1 lb cooked beef or mutton	beef bones
1 small carrot	½ teacup mushroom
½ small turnip	ketchup
1 scant tablespoon flour	seasoning
½ teaspoon Yorkshire relish	1 bunch of mixed herbs
or similar sauce	or some parsley, thyme
1 small onion	and a bayleaf

Slice the meat thinly. Using a pint of water, make a stock with the bones, vegetables and herbs—cook together for 1½ hours.

Melt some dripping. Peel and chop the onion and fry until brown. Stir in the flour gradually. Keep stirring and add the mushroom ketchup, sauce and seasoning. Add the strained stock a little at a time and stirring well. Put in the meat slices and heat thoroughly.

Pound Cake from Bradford

12 oz S.R. flour	1 lemon
8 oz butter or margarine	4 eggs
8 oz sugar	

Beat the sugar and butter together until very light. Whisk the eggs and add to the mixture alternately with the flour but a little at a time. Grate the rind from the lemon and add, together with the juice. Put into a well greased tin and bake at 325 until firm, about 1¾ hours.

At Leeds and Bradford, young people walked up Beamsley Beacon every Easter Sunday morning, to see the sun dance at dawn. It is traditional throughout the north for people to walk to a high point at this time, although the reason behind it has been forgotten and now the walk is often made on Good Friday. It is a very ancient custom arising from the belief that the sun dances as it rises above the horizon, in honour of the Resurrection. An old ballad contains these lines—

'But Dick, she dances such a way!
No sun upon an Easter Day
Is half so fine a sight.'

Harrogate Tart

3 egg yolks	4 drops almond essence
1 whole egg	1 pint hot milk
2 oz castor sugar	a little cold milk
3 oz plain flour	1 oz butter
3 oz ground almonds	

Mix the flour to a smooth paste with cold milk then stir in the yolks, one at a time. Mix in the whole, beaten egg and the sugar, stirring very thoroughly. Cut the butter into small pieces and mix into the hot milk then very gradually stir this into the egg mixture. Put the bowl over a pan of hot water, or empty the contents into a double saucepan and cook. Stir constantly, until the mixture is like thick cream. Do not allow it to boil. When thick, remove from the heat and beat in the ground almonds and essence. Pour into a baked, pastry flan case and serve with fresh cream. The filling can also be used to cover a fruit-filled flan.

Pancakes

4 oz plain flour	1 egg
$\frac{1}{3}$ pint of milk	a good pinch of salt

Mix together the flour and salt. Beat the egg with half the milk and stir this gradually into the flour, using a wooden spoon. Beat to a smooth batter and stir in the remaining milk, a little at a time. Heat a frying pan, put in a small knob of fat and melt. When it is quite hot pour in enough batter to cover the bottom of the pan. When cooked, turn and cook the other side. Serve with lemon juice and castor sugar.

Pancakes are traditionally eaten on Shrove Tuesday which is the day before the beginning of Lent. In the past, everyone went to church on this day to be shriven of their sins. Since fasting was strictly adhered to during Lent, all the fats in the house were used up beforehand in the cooking of pancakes.

In some areas, the first pancake was often thrown out to the hens, the number coming to eat was supposed to show the number of years which would pass before the cook would marry.

Parliament Street, Harrogate, in June 1919. This would be a year of relief after the ending of the 1914-18 war and the fashionably dressed crowd, with the ladies mostly carrying parasols to protect their complexions from the sun, are far removed from its' horrors. Predominant on an advertisement for the theatre during the August Bank Holiday week is the name of Harry Lauder. Bath-chairs are greatly in evidence, for Harrogate at that time was a very fashionable spa resort.

The small boy in the left foreground is carrying a big basket and selling what could be song-sheets. Both coachmen with carriages and chauffeurs with cars are meeting their employers as they emerge from the 'Kursaal'. Although by present day standards there is very little traffic, a policeman is on point duty.

A photograph taken in Settle at the start of the First World War, showing horses being led away for use in the army.

West Riding Pudding

6 oz shortcrust pastry	2 eggs
2 tablespoons red jam	4 oz butter
1 oz ground almonds	4 oz S.R. flour
4 oz castor sugar	the grated rind of $\frac{1}{2}$ lemon

Line a shallow dish with the pastry. Decorate the edges and spread jam on the base. Cream the butter and sugar until light then beat in the eggs gradually. Sift together the dry ingredients and fold these in without beating. Cover the jam with this mixture and bake in a moderate oven, 350 Mark 4 for 35-45 minutes until well risen and firm. Dust with castor sugar.

Rowan Jelly

The old recipe I took this from described it as being a 'beautiful, rich red colour' and having a 'delicately smoky aroma'. It is perhaps more accurately described as sharply bitter and I think a pleasanter flavour is obtained from a combination of rowan berries and crab apples. Use half of each, or a greater proportion of apples.

Rowan jelly was traditionally served with mountain mutton or lamb. Lamb from the valleys being served with the red currants that grew in those areas.

Rowan berries
sugar
crab apples

Put the fruit into a pan and well cover with water. Boil to a pulp and strain through a fine cloth. Measure the juice and return to the pan with a pound of sugar to each pint. Boil for 10 minuutes, or until a little sets when tested. Pot while hot.

Settle is a typical, small market town of the West Riding which has retained much of its' character because it has not suffered from over-enthusiastic developers. Many old traditions have survived in towns and villages like Settle, but one which died out at the end of the century was that which took place on December 21st., St. Thomas's Day. This custom was for poor widows, or other women who would not normally beg, to go from house to house where they were given food or small measures of wheat. This was known as 'going a-Thomasing' or 'going a-gooding' and was probably remembered by some of the people on the photograph.

A print of the Market Place, Beverley in 1830. Although this is obviously market day, the general impression is of a leisurely way of life. Markets were much more important in the community in those days and shopping was part of a social event.

There is a record of 34 lb of sugar being bought in Richmond in 1176 for the kings' use. It cost 9d a pound which was extremely expensive, but it was a great luxury then.

Beverley Spiced Beef

Use a piece of beef skirting at least 1½ lb in weight and rub it well with dry salt. Leave overnight and drain next day then wipe over with a clean cloth. Mix together a little ground cloves and black pepper and rub this into the beef. Roll it up tightly and tie securely with string. Put into a pan with water, or preferably stock, to cover and bring to the boil. Reduce the heat, cover and simmer gently for 2½ hours or longer, depending on the size. A chopped onion and carrot can also be added to improve the flavour. Remove the beef when cooked and leave under a weighted board to press until next day. Cut off the string and serve sliced. This is a very tasty way of using a cheap cut of beef and is delicious, not only with salad and other cold dishes but with savoury stuffed baked potatoes and freshly made pickled onions. A bonus to this dish is the liquid in which the beef was cooked, which can be sieved and served as a very good clear soup or, after sieving, long grain rice or pasta added. Otherwise it makes an excellent stock for a special soup.

Mushroom Ketchup

½ lb mushrooms
1 oz salt
a pinch each of ground ginger, ground mace, black pepper and white pepper.

Rinse the mushrooms in boiling water. Drain well and dab dry. Put under a very low heat to dry further. Place half in a stoneware jar, sprinkle with half the salt, add the remaining mushrooms and finally the salt. Cover and leave three days, stirring two or three times each day. Put into a lidded jar on the hob for a day—or in a cool oven 200 for 1½ hours.

Strain the liquid through muslin into a pan, add all the spices and seasonings. Cover and simmer gently for 20 minutes. When cold, put into a bottle and cover tightly.

This is adapted from a very old recipe and is used in a lot of old savoury dishes.

Paradise Squares

4 oz butter	2 oz glace cherries
4 oz caster sugar	1 egg
2 oz ground rice	1 cup of sultanas
2 oz chopped walnuts	shortcrust pastry

Line a shallow 8″ square tin with the pastry. Cream the butter and sugar, beat the egg and mix in with the ground rice. Stir in the nuts and fruit and put the mixture into the prepared tin, smooth the top and bake at 400 until golden brown on top. Remove from the oven and while still warm, sprinkle with sugar. Cut into squares when cold.

This is taken from an old Wolds farm recipe book and was given to me by the compiler of the booklet to commemorate Beverley's 400th anniversary of the Charter. This was presented by Queen Elizabeth I on July 24th 1573, giving the town the right to a Mayor and 12 Aldermen.

Pateley Bridge 1905
A narrow, cobbled street well endowed with hotels but obviously catering for different sections of the community.

The cart carrying a milk churn is a reminder that milk was then sold by the measure, in the housewives own jug or basin.

Pepper Cake (a recipe from Pateley Bridge)

12 oz plain flour
12 oz black treacle
4 oz butter or margarine

2 beaten eggs
4 oz soft brown sugar
½ oz ground cloves
½ teaspoon pearl ash or bicarbonate of soda

Rub the fat into the flour, add the sugar and spice. Mix the ash or bicarbonate of soda with a little milk and add to the flour with the treacle and eggs. Mix all together thoroughly and put into a well greased and lined tin. Bake until firm in a moderate oven 50 to 60 minutes.

This was a Christmas speciality, given to carol-singers and any visitor. The Christmas Waits often ended their singing with the verse.

'A little bit of pepper cake,
A little bit of cheese.
A little drink of water
And a penny, if you please!

Yorkshire Toad

Yorkshire Pudding mixture.
1 lb pork sausages
Melt some dripping in a deep baking tin and leave in the oven 450° gas Mark 7 until hot. Pour in the batter and spread the sausages evenly in this, then bake until crisply brown—about 45 minutes.

This tends to be slightly fatty, so if you prefer something drier, heat the sausages gently in water to cover, then simmer for a few minutes to extract some of the fat.

The three Ridings of Yorkshire (disregarding the disorganisation caused by the new reorganisation) are of Danish and Norse origin. They were originally divisions made for Government administration, the smallest ones were Wapentakes (Weapon-shakes) and all males who were able to 'shake a weapon' or bear arms were allowed to attend meetings and to vote, 'Things' were larger assemblies with delegates from the smaller Wapentakes attending. Similarly, the Great Things were the biggest meetings with delegates from the 'Things'. This was perhaps the equivalent of our Parliament.

In time, 'Things' became not only the meetings but the name was also used for the divisions from which representatives were selected. Each third of the county was known as a 'Thri-thing' and it is easy to see how this became corrupted to T'Ridings.

The Rolls of Parliament for 1474 record 'The Shire of York in the Estrithing, Northrithing and Westrithing of the same . . .'.

Station Road, Doncaster in 1903, with everyone appearing to be interested in the photographer. Oddly, the only traffic in the road is four trams.

Doncaster Butterscotch

1 lb sugar	6 oz butter
½ pint milk	a pinch of cream of tartar

Put the sugar and milk into a large pan and heat gently until the sugar dissolves. Add the butter cut into small pieces. As it melts, stir in the cream of tartar. Bring to the boil and boil hard until soft ball stage (sets firmly but soft—not brittle, when tested by dropping a little into cold water). Pour into a well buttered tin to set.

Yorkshire Savoury Pudding

½ lb bread	1 oz oatmeal
4 oz shredded suet	1 or 2 teaspoons of sage
4 large onions	seasoning

Pour boiling water over the bread and leave for 30 minutes. Strain and mix with the oatmeal. Powder the sage, chop the onion and mix into the bread with seasoning. Heat the oven to 425° or Mark 5, put the mixture into a greased tin and bake until brown. This will take approximately 50 minutes. Slice and serve with thick gravy with the meat.

Between Doncaster and Pontefract is the village of Barnsdale which is associated with many legends of Robin Hood, for it was in the forest here that he hid after first becoming outlawed. In the old ballad of Robin Hood and the Bishop of Hereford is the verse—

'Then Robin he took the Bishop by the hand
And led him to merry Barnsdale;
He made him to stay and sup with him that night,
And to drink wine, beer and ale'.

The imposing Victoria Square, Hull as seen in 1904.

An odd custom took place in Hull up to the mid-nineteenth century. It was common practice each year on Oct. 10th to whip any dogs which were roaming the streets and children especially felt it was a duty to make a whip ready for that day. In 1853, however, was written 'This custom is now obsolete, the new police having effectually stopped the cruel pastime of the Hull boys.'

This custom was also followed in York on St. Lukes Day, October 18th.

Brandy Snaps

Brandy snaps have been connected with Hull Fair for many decades. The Fair dates back to a time when Hull was called Wyke. Its' name was changed to Kingston-upon-Hull in 1293, but the Fair was first held in 1279.

2 oz butter	1 teaspoon brandy
2 oz sugar	1 level teaspoon ground ginger
2 oz flour	$\frac{1}{4}$ teaspoon grated lemon rind
2 tablesppons syrup	

Melt the butter, syrup and sugar in a pan. Remove from the heat and add the other ingrdeints. Mix well and drop in teaspoons on a greased baking sheet. Space about 3″ apart as they spread during cooking. Bake 350° about 7 minutes or until they are light brown and set. Allow to cool on the sheet for two minutes then loosen with a palette knife. Remove and roll each one quickly around the handle of a wooden spoon to shape.

Westgate, Wakefield in 1904, a year in which there were 190 deaths and 22,500 accidents on the roads of the country caused by horse-drawn vehicles and 13 people killed by cars.

Wakefield Pudding

1 lb apples	¾ pint water
2 oz sugar	stale bread

Peel, core and cut up the apples. Stew in the water with the sugar until soft. Line a buttered basin with some of the bread and put some apple on the bottom, then alternate layers of bread and fruit until the basin is full. The top layer must be bread. Put a plate over that just fits inside the basin rim. Place a weight on top and leave in a cold place overnight. Turn out, sprinkle with sugar and serve with cream.

This is apparently a version of the traditional English Summer Pudding which can be made as follows—

1 lb raspberries	4 oz sugar
4 oz redcurrants	

Stew the ingredients together until the sugar melts, then for a further two or three minutes. Keep the lid on the pan all the time. Allow to cool. Line a basin with slices of day-old bread without crusts. Leave no gaps in the bread. Fill with the fruit but keep back some juice. Cover with a lid of bread and a plate as for Wakefield Pudding. Weigh and leave overnight. Turn out and pour over the extra juice. Sprinkle with sugar and serve with thick, fresh cream. There is a lot of juice with this Pudding, so use a deep dish to turn out.

Knaresborough Marketplace in 1904.
A very attractive square with bow-fronted shops and cobblestones.

Knaresborough Picnic Pie

Line a pie-dish with flaky or shortcrust pastry. Cover this with cold, tender boiled ham, then a layer of unbeaten, raw eggs—keep the yolks whole. Add seasoning to taste. Repeat the layers until the dish is full, ending with a layer of ham. Cover with pastry and bake in a moderate oven until golden brown.

Yorkshire Fat Rascals

1 lb plain flour	2 oz brown sugar
8oz butter	salt
4 oz currants	

Rub the butter into the flour, add the currants, sugar and salt. Mix in enough milk and water to make a slack dough. Roll out to $\frac{1}{2}''$ thick, cut into rounds and dust with icing sugar. Put on a greased baking tin and bake in a moderately hot oven until lightly browned.

Market Day in Richmond at the beginning of the century, showing a variety of unattended carts.

King Arthur and his knights are said to be in a spell-bound sleep beneath the foundations of the great tower in Richmond. A local man, Potter Thompson, long ago found his way into the vault and saw all the men around a great table on which lay a horn and a sword in a scabbard. About to draw the sword, he saw the sleepers were stirring and hastily went out, but as he did he heard a voice call—

'Potter Potter Thompson
If thou hadst either drawn
The sword or blown the horn,
Thou'd been the luckiest man
That ever was born.'

Lambs Wool from Richmond

This is a very old type of punch, traditionally served at Christmas-time in Yorkshire and other parts of the north. It is made with hot, strong ale, apple-pulp and spices. The wool was of course represented by the soft apple pulp, which floated on the top of the punch.

The apples were first roasted by the fire (they could now be baked in the oven) and the pulp scooped from the cooked fruit. Sometimes crab apples were used and instead of having the pulp taken out, they were, after roasting, floated whole on the top of the hot, spiced ale.

Saltburn-by-the-sea about 1920.

Kidney Soup (a recipe from Saltburn)

4 oz shin beef
4 oz beef kidney
1 small onion
finely chopped parsley
or 1 teaspoon dried
2 medium sized carrots
3½ pints of good stock
2 tablespoons barley

2 level tablespoons cornflour
seasoning
a pinch of nutmeg and 1 bay leaf
(both optional)

Chop the beef and kidney finely. Melt the butter and brown the meat in it then the finely chopped onion. Add the peeled, chopped carrot, the stock, barley and all the seasonings etc. Cover and simmer for 2 hours. Remove the bayleaf. Blend the cornflour with a little cold water in a bowl and pour into the simmering soup. Bring to the boil, then reduce the heat. Cover and cook for 15 minutes.

If preferred, the soup can be sieved before adding the cornflour.

Custard Pie

Custard pie was a traditional dish for Easter Sunday tea in many parts of Yorkshire and especially in the Whitby area, where the name 'custard wind' was given to an easterly wind prevalent there during the Easter period.

6 oz shortcrust pastry $\frac{1}{2}$ pint milk
2 eggs   a few drops vanille essence
2 oz sugar   grated nutmeg

Line a greased flan tin or pie-dish with the pastry. Whisk the eggs and milk well together and stir in the sugar and essence. Strain into the pastry case and sprinkle on the nutmeg. Bake in a hot oven 425-450 for 10 minutes then turn down to 350 and cook until firm.

Whitby harbour, which saw the departure of James Cook as an apprentice on his first ship and later was to provide for his great voyages of discovery.

The subsidy roll for Whitby in 1301 listed weavers, dyers, masons, bakers, cooks, brewers, skinners, barbers, grocers, fowlers, one shoemaker and one goldsmith working in the town. The man William the Goldsmith was one of only three of that craft working in Yorkshire at that time.

Whitby Fish Pie

Steam some white fish and remove all the bones, skin etc. Cut some lean, raw ham into small pieces. Slice some hard-bloiled eggs. Butter a pie-dish and fill it with alternate layers of the above three ingredients. Moisten with a little of the liquor from the fish. When the dish is full, cover with shortcrust pastry and bake in a hot oven until the pastry is done.

Oatcakes

Oatcakes have been traditional in Yorkshire for centuries, oats being the staple food in hilly areas. The oats were ground locally then the meal was stored in a wooden ark in the home. It was pressed down very firmly or even stamped down.

A visitor to Skipton in 1797 wrote "Oatmeal is made into bread and sometimes into hasty pudding".

In a book of 1674, several words were used for oatcakes. They were called tharve-cakes, riddle-cakes and clapbread. They have also been known as havercake or haverbread in some places.

In 1805, a man writing about Linton in Wharfedale said "They all grew oats, which formed the principal article of their subsistence; the kiln in which the grain was parched previous to its being ground belonged to the township at large, and when in use was a sort of village coffee-house where the politics of the place and the day were discussed. Of oatmeal their bread was invariably made and most of the puddings; and this, mixed with milk or water when milk was scarce, supplied them with breakfast and supper''.

The oatcakes were cooked on a stone or iron backstone. This was either built over a small, closed-in fire, rested on the open fire or placed on the oven bottom. The making of stone backstones could only take place in certain areas where mudstone occurred. It was recorded as early as the 15th century. The stone was hand quarried and when a large piece was removed it was immediately placed in the nearest stream to be covered in water. This prevented the shaley stone from breaking up. The stone was later split into inch thick slabs and one side dressed before putting the slab beside a fire to harden. When cooled, the stones were carried from town to town on packhorses. About twenty backstones made up a load.

To make oatcakes, a batter was made in a wooden kneading trough or 'knade-kit'. Oatmeal and water or butter-milk were mixed together. A riddle or backboard (a square board with a handle, often made of oak) was sprinkled with oatmeal. The batter was dropped onto the meal and 'reeled' into shape by shaking the board with both hands. It was next drawn onto a piece of flannel or muslin on another board and from this was tossed onto the backstone.

Variations did occur in the making of oatcakes, most people had some 'secret' method to include which gave their oatcakes superiority but I have given the general method which was used. I am told that the following recipes give similar results.

1. 1 pint mixed milk and water
   1 oz yeast
   6 oz fine oatmeal
   3 oz plain flour
   1 scant teaspoon salt

Mix the flour, salt and oatmeal. Warm the liquid and stir in gradually to make a smooth batter. Crumble in the yeast, stir gently and leave to stand in a warm place for 20 minutes. Stir again and cook in a strong, well-greased frying pan. Pour in enough batter to cover the base fairly thinly and turn out when cooked.

2. 1 pint warm water
   $\frac{1}{2}$ oz bread yeast
   $1\frac{1}{2}$ lb fine oatmeal

Stir together all the ingredients and mix gently with your hands until smooth. Cover and leave in a warm place to prove for half an hour. This mixture was used to bind together coarser oatmeal and the simplest method appeared to be as follows.

Cover a board with coarse, dry oatmeal. Pour on some batter to cover the oatmeal, shake into shape then throw the oatcake into a long oval on the heated backstone or whatever is used.

When cooked, the oatcakes were hung on plain wooden racks suspended from the ceiling. These were called bread fleaks. The oatcakes were then eaten either fresh or dried. Fried with bacon or buttered and eaten alone or with cheese, treacle, etc. My preference is for fresh oatcakes, well buttered and spread with a good layer of treacle—delicious.

Squab Pie

2 lb best neck end of lamb
4 small onions
1½ lb dessert apples
¼ pint of stock

the grated rind of 1 lemon
seasoning
a good pinch of nutmeg
1 level teaspoon cinnamon

Cut the meat from the bones and remove the skin. Cut into small pieces. Peel, core and slice the apples. Peel and chop the onions. Grease a dish and put in the meat, apple and onion. Sprinkle in the spices and seasoning. Cover with pastry or a layer of thinly sliced potatoes. Bake in a moderate oven for 375°, Mark 5 for 1½ hours. If the pastry is getting too brown, cover with a piece of brown paper or a double layer of greaseproof paper.

Rice Pudding

Walter White wrote in 1861 "I came to Buckden, the next village, just in time to dine with the haymakers. Right good fare was provided—roast mutton, salad and rice pudding. Who would not be a haymaker!"

A recipe from 1748—Take a quarter of a pound of rice and put it into a saucepan with a quart of new milk, a stick of cinnamon. Stir it often to keep it from sticking to the saucepan. When it is boiled thick pour it into a pan stir in a quarter of a pound of fresh butter and sugar to your taste (four ounces). Grate half a nutmeg, add three or four spoonfuls of rosewater and stir all together. When it is cold beat up eight eggs and four whites and beat it all together. Butter dish and pour it all in and bake it.

Mint Jelly

1 oz gelatine
½ pint vinegar

1 lb sugar
4 tablespoons chopped mint

Melt the gelatine in half a cup of warm water. Boil the sugar and vinegar together for 5 minutes. Cool slightly then stir in all the ingredients together. Pour into small moulds.

Fine Fritters 1748

Put to half a pint of thick cream four eggs well beaten, a a little brandy, some nutmeg and ginger. Make this into a thick batter with flour; mix all together and fry in butter.

In 1782, a young clergyman came to England from Germany to visit the birthplace of his favourite poet Milton. He wrote in a letter to a friend 'The slices of bread and butter which they give you with your tea, are as thin as poppy leaves. But there is another kind of bread and butter usually eaten with tea, which is toasted by the fire and is incomparably good. You take one slice after the other, and hold it to the fire on a fork till the butter is melted, so that it penetrates a number of slices at once: this is called toast.'

Beef dripping, well creamed with a little thin mustard, is better than butter for beef sandwiches.

A Yorkshire Lullaby

Rock a boo babby, babbies es bonny.
Two in a creddle, three es ta monny,
Four es a compnay, five es a charge,
Six es a family, seven's ta large.

Halifax High Tea Beef

4 lb piece of salted brisket of beef	seasoning
$\frac{1}{2}$ lb bacon pieces	a good pinch of each of ground cloves, allspice and ground mace
2 carrots	
1 onion	a bunch of savoury herbs

Put all the ingredients into an oven dish and cover with water. Put on a tightly fitting lid and cook gently in the oven (300-325) for 4 hours. Leave in the liquid to cool. Remove, put on a dish, place a plate on top with a heavy weight on that. Leave overnight to press.

A Good Soup from Leeds

2 oz butter	$\frac{1}{2}$ lb carrots
2 oz lentils	a pinch of sugar
3 pints light stock	fresh, chopped parsley
1 medium sized onion	of $\frac{1}{2}$ a teaspoon dried
1 oz barley	parsley

Melt 1 oz of the butter in a pan. Chop the peeled onion finely and cook slowly in the butter until golden. Peel and chop the carrots finely and add with the remaining butter. Stir over a low heat for a few minutes. Add the stock and all the other ingredients. Season well, bring to the boil then reduce the heat. Cover and simmer approximately $1\frac{1}{2}$ hours. Add the parsley 10 minutes before serving.